Country Classics

PREFACE

Learning to play a musical instrument is one of the most satisfying experiences a person can have. Being able to play along with other musicians makes that even more rewarding. This collection of classic country songs is designed to make it easy to enjoy the fun of gathering with friends and family to make music together.

The selections in this book include a variety of songs drawn from several decades of country music. From Hank Williams, Sr. to Alan Jackson, these songs will provide fun opportunities to make music with other players. The music for each song displays the chord diagrams for five instruments: ukulele, baritone ukulele, guitar, mandolin and banjo. The chord diagrams indicate basic, commonly used finger positions. More advanced players can substitute alternate chord formations.

It's easy to find recordings of all these tunes performed by outstanding musicians. Listening to multiple versions by creative artists can help you to understand the choices you can make about style as you and your friends play these songs.

Arranged by Mark Phillips

ISBN 978-1-5400-6411-0

Visit Hal Leonard Online at
www.halleonard.com

Contact us:
Hal Leonard
7777 West Bluemound Road
Milwaukee, WI 53213
Email: info@halleonard.com

In Europe, contact:
Hal Leonard Europe Limited
42 Wigmore Street
Marylebone, London, W1U 2RN
Email: info@halleonardeurope.com

In Australia, contact:
Hal Leonard Australia Pty. Ltd.
4 Lentara Court
Cheltenham, Victoria, 3192 Australia
Email: info@halleonard.com.au

MW00852450

Standard Ukulele

A    E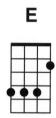

Baritone Ukulele

A    E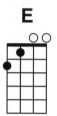

Guitar

A 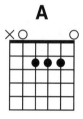   E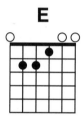

Mandolin

A 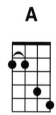   E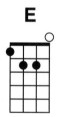

Banjo

A    E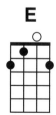

Achy Breaky Heart
(Don't Tell My Heart)
Words and Music by Don Von Tress

Verse
Moderately

1. You can tell the world you nev-er was my girl.
2. You can tell my arms go back to the farm.
3., 4. *See additional lyrics*

You can burn my clothes when I'm gone. Or
You can tell my feet to hit the floor. Or

you can tell your friends just what a fool I've been and
you can tell my lips to tell my fin-ger-tips and they

laugh and joke a-bout me on the phone.
won't be reach-ing out for you no more.

Chorus

Don't tell my heart, my ach-y break-y heart. I just don't think he'd un-der-

stand. And if you tell my heart, my ach-y break-y heart, he

To Coda

D.C. al Coda (take repeat)

Coda

might blow up and kill this man.

man.

Additional Lyrics

3. You can tell your ma I moved to Arkansas.
   You can tell your dog to bite my leg.
   Or tell your brother Cliff, whose fist can tell my lip.
   He never really liked me anyway.

4. Or tell your Aunt Louise, tell anything you please.
   Myself already knows I'm not okay.
   Or you can tell my eyes to watch out for my mind.
   It might be walking out on me today. But…

Standard Ukulele

A	E7	Bm7	F°7	B7

Baritone Ukulele

A	E7	Bm7	F°7	B7

Guitar

A	E7	Bm7	F°7	B7

Mandolin

A	E7	Bm7	F°7	B7

Banjo

A	E7	Bm7	F°7	B7

All My Ex's Live in Texas

Words and Music by Lyndia J. Shafer and Sanger D. Shafer

7

Standard Ukulele

G D Em C C#m7b5 Am Dsus4

Baritone Ukulele

G D Em C C#m7b5 Am Dsus4

Guitar

G D Em C 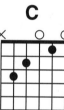 C#m7b5 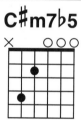 Am Dsus4

Mandolin

G D  Em C C#m7b5 Am Dsus4

Banjo

G D Em C C#m7b5 Am Dsus4

Always on My Mind

Words and Music by Wayne Thompson, Mark James and Johnny Christopher

Standard Ukulele

C	G7	C7	F	D7
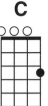		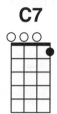	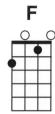	

Baritone Ukulele

C	G7	C7	F	D7
	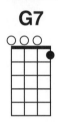			

Guitar

C	G7	C7	F	D7
	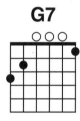	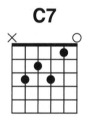		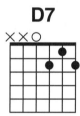

Mandolin

C	G7	C7	F	D7
		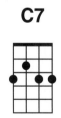		

Banjo

C	G7	C7	F	D7
	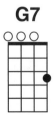			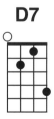

Back in the Saddle Again

Words and Music by Gene Autry and Ray Whitley

Standard Ukulele

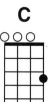 C
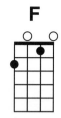 F
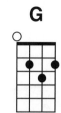 G
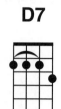 D7
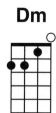 Dm
 Em

Baritone Ukulele

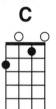 C
 F
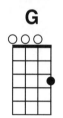 G
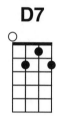 D7
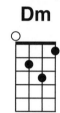 Dm
 Em

Guitar

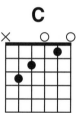 C
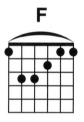 F
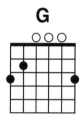 G
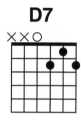 D7
 Dm
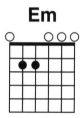 Em

Mandolin

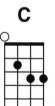 C
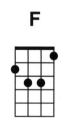 F
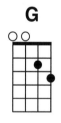 G
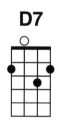 D7
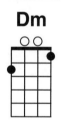 Dm
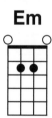 Em

Banjo

 C
 F
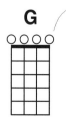 G
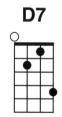 D7
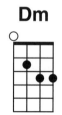 Dm
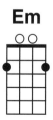 Em

Behind Closed Doors

Words and Music by Kenny O'Dell

Standard Ukulele

D	A7	D7	G	Gm6

Baritone Ukulele

D	A7	D7	G	Gm6

Guitar

D	A7	D7	G	Gm6

Mandolin

D	A7	D7	G	Gm6

Banjo

D	A7	D7	G	Gm6

Blue Bayou

Words and Music by Roy Orbison and Joe Melson

Standard Ukulele

E	B7	A

Baritone Ukulele

E	B7	A

Guitar

E	B7	A

Mandolin

E	B7	A

Banjo

E	B7	A

Blue Eyes Crying in the Rain

Words and Music by Fred Rose

Verse
Moderately slow, in 2

1. In the twi-light glow I see her,
2. Now my hair has turned to sil - ver;

blue eyes cry-ing in the rain.
all my life I've loved in vain.

As we kissed good-bye and part - ed, I
I can see her star in heav - en,

knew we'd nev-er meet a - gain.
blue eyes cry - ing in the rain.

Love is like a dy-ing em - ber;
Some - day when we meet up yon - der,

on - ly mem-o-ries re - main.
we'll stroll hand in hand a - gain

Through the ag - es I'll re - mem - ber
in a land that knows no part - ing.

blue eyes cry - ing in the rain.
Blue eyes cry - ing in the rain.

Standard Ukulele

D	G	A

Baritone Ukulele

D	G	A
	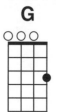	

Guitar

D	G	A
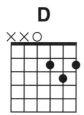	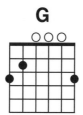	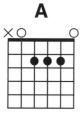

Mandolin

D	G	A
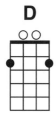	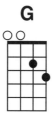	

Banjo

D	G	A
	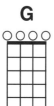	

Boot Scootin' Boogie

Words and Music by Ronnie Dunn

Additional Lyrics

2. I got a good job; I work hard for my money.
   When it's quittin' time, I hit the door runnin'.
   I fire up my pickup truck and let the horses run.
   I go flyin' down that highway to that hideaway
   Stuck out in the woods to do the boot scootin' boogie.

3. The bartender asks me, says, "Son, what'll it be?"
   I want a shot at that redhead yonder lookin' at me.
   The dance floor's hoppin' and it's hotter than the Fourth of July.
   I see outlaws, inlaws, crooks and straights,
   All out makin' it shake, doin' the boot scootin' boogie.

Standard Ukulele

C	G	F	D
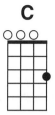	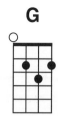		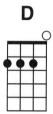

Baritone Ukulele

C	G	F	D
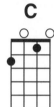			

Guitar

C	G	F	D
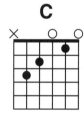	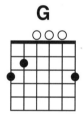		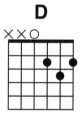

Mandolin

C	G	F	D
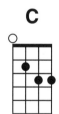	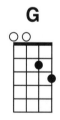		

Banjo

C	G	F	D
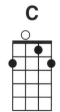	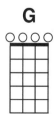		

Chattahoochee

Words and Music by Jim McBride and Alan Jackson

Standard Ukulele

D	A7	G

Baritone Ukulele

D	A7	G

Guitar

D	A7	G

Mandolin

D	A7	G

Banjo

D	A7	G

Cold, Cold Heart

Words and Music by Hank Williams

Standard Ukulele

A	A7	D	E	E7sus4	Dm
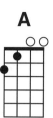			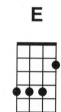	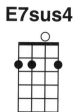	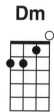

Baritone Ukulele

A	A7	D	E	E7sus4	Dm
			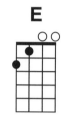	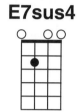	

Guitar

A	A7	D	E	E7sus4	Dm
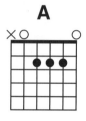		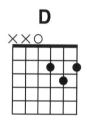			

Mandolin

A	A7	D	E	E7sus4	Dm
	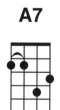	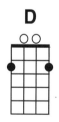		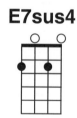	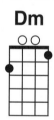

Banjo

A	A7	D	E	E7sus4	Dm
				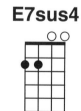	

Could I Have This Dance

Words and Music by Wayland Holyfield and Bob House

Standard Ukulele

A	E	E7	A7	D
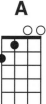				

Baritone Ukulele

A	E	E7	A7	D

Guitar

A	E	E7	A7	D
		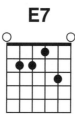		

Mandolin

A	E	E7	A7	D
	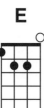	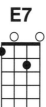		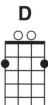

Banjo

A	E	E7	A7	D

Cryin' Time

Words and Music by Buck Owens

Standard Ukulele

C   **G7**

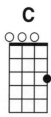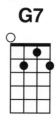

Baritone Ukulele

C   **G7**

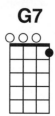

Guitar

C   **G7**

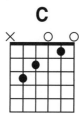

Mandolin

C   **G7**

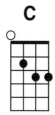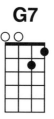

Banjo

C   **G7**

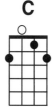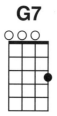

Deep in the Heart of Texas

Words by June Hershey
Music by Don Swander

Standard Ukulele

E	A	B7

Baritone Ukulele

E	A	B7

Guitar

E	A	B7

Mandolin

E	A	B7

Banjo

E	A	B7

Folsom Prison Blues

Words and Music by John R. Cash

1. I hear the train a com-in', it's roll-in' 'round the bend, ___ and
I was just a ba-by, my ma-ma, told me, "Son, ___
bet there's rich folks eat-in' in a fan-cy din-ing car. ___ They're
freed me from this pris-on, if that rail-road train was mine, ___ I

I ain't seen the sun - shine since I don't ___ know when. I'm
al - ways be a good ___ boy; don't ev - er play ___ with guns." But I
prob' - ly drink - in' cof - fee and smok - ing big ___ ci - gars. Well, I
bet I'd move it on ___ a lit - tle far - ther down ___ the line.

stuck in Fol - som Pri - son, and time keeps drag - gin' on. ___
shot a man in Re - no just to watch him die. ___
know I had it com - in'; I know I can't be free. ___
Far from Fol - som Pri - son, that's where I want to stay. ___

But that train keeps a roll - in'
When I hear that whis - tle blow - in',
But those peo - ple keep a mov - in'
And I'd let that lone - some whis - tle

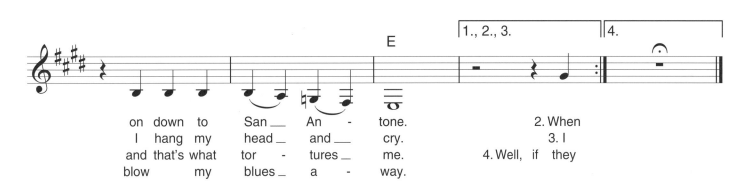

on down to San ___ An - tone.   2. When
I hang my head ___ and ___ cry.   3. I
and that's what tor - tures ___ me.   4. Well, if they
blow my blues a - way.

Standard Ukulele

Am	D	G	C	G7	Cm	F#°7
	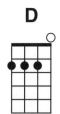	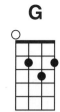	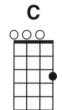	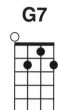		

Baritone Ukulele

Am	D	G	C	G7	Cm	F#°7
	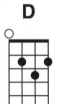	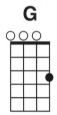	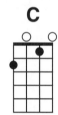	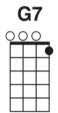		

Guitar

Am	D	G	C	G7	Cm	F#°7
	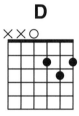	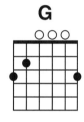	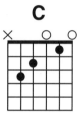		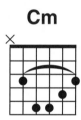	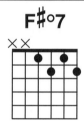

Mandolin

Am	D	G	C	G7	Cm	F#°7
	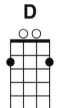	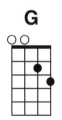	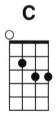	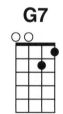	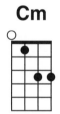	

Banjo

Am	D	G	C	G7	Cm	F#°7
		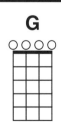		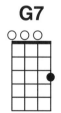		

For the Good Times

Words and Music by Kris Kristofferson

Standard Ukulele

G	G7	Am7	D7	C

Baritone Ukulele

G	G7	Am7	D7	C

Guitar

G	G7	Am7	D7	C

  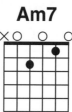

Mandolin

G	G7	Am7	D7	C

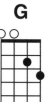 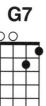

Banjo

G	G7	Am7	D7	C

 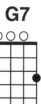

Four Walls

Words and Music by Marvin J. Moore and George H. Campbell, Jr.

Standard Ukulele

A	A#°7	Bm	E	Dm

Baritone Ukulele

A	A#°7	Bm	E	Dm

Guitar

A	A#°7	Bm	E	Dm

Mandolin

A	A#°7	Bm	E	Dm

Banjo

A	A#°7	Bm	E	Dm

Friends in Low Places

Words and Music by DeWayne Blackwell and Earl Bud Lee

Standard Ukulele

E	A	E7	F♯7	B7

Baritone Ukulele

E	A	E7	F♯7	B7

Guitar

E	A	E7	F♯7	B7
		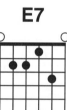		

Mandolin

E	A	E7	F♯7	B7

Banjo

E	A	E7	F♯7	B7

Funny How Time Slips Away

Words and Music by Willie Nelson

Standard Ukulele

D	Dmaj7	D6	Em	Em(maj7)	Em7	A7

Baritone Ukulele

D	Dmaj7	D6	Em	Em(maj7)	Em7	A7
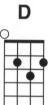	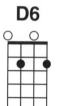	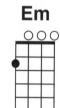	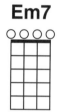			

Guitar

D	Dmaj7	D6	Em	Em(maj7)	Em7	A7
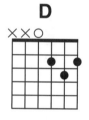		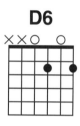		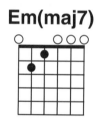		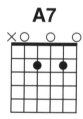

Mandolin

D	Dmaj7	D6	Em	Em(maj7)	Em7	A7
	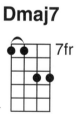	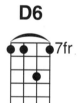		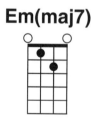		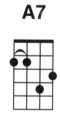

Banjo

D	Dmaj7	D6	Em	Em(maj7)	Em7	A7
			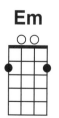	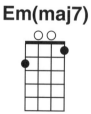	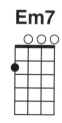	

Gentle on My Mind

Words and Music by John Hartford

Verse
Moderately, in 2

1. It's know-ing that your door is al-ways o-pen and your path is free to
   cling-ing to the rocks and i-vy plant-ed on their col-umns now that
3., 4. *See additional lyrics*

walk
bind me,
that makes me tend to leave my sleep-ing
or some-thing that some-bod-y said be-

bag rolled up and stashed be-hind your couch.
cause they thought we fit to-geth-er walk-ing.

And it's know-ing I'm not shack-led by for-got-ten words and bonds and the
It's just know-ing that the world will not be curs-ing or for-giv-ing when I

ink stains that have dried up-on some line that
walk a-long some rail-road track and find that you're

keeps you in the back roads by the riv-ers of my mem-'ry, that keeps you ev-er
mov-ing on the back roads by the riv-ers of my mem-'ry and for ho-urs you're just

gen-tle on my mind.

2. It's not
3. Though the
4. I

Additional Lyrics

3. Though the wheat fields and the clotheslines
   And the junkyards and the highways come between us,
   And some other woman's crying to her mother
   'Cause she turned and I was gone,
   I still might run in silence, tears of joy might stain my face,
   And the summer sun might burn me till I'm blind,
   But not to where I cannot see
   You walkin' on the back roads
   By the rivers flowing gentle on my mind.

4. I dip my cup of soup back from a
   Gurgling, crackling cauldron in some train yard,
   My beard a rustling coal pile,
   And a dirty hat pulled low across my face.
   Through cupped hands 'round a tin can
   I pretend to hold you to my breast and find
   That you're waiting from the back roads
   By the rivers of my memory,
   Ever smiling, ever gentle on my mind.

Standard Ukulele

C	F	Dm	B♭	G	Em	Am
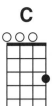	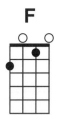					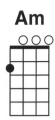

Baritone Ukulele

C	F	Dm	B♭	G	Em	Am
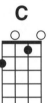				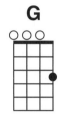	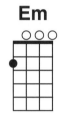	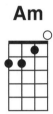

Guitar

C	F	Dm	B♭	G	Em	Am
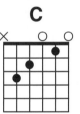		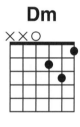	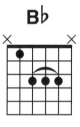			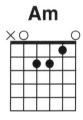

Mandolin

C	F	Dm	B♭	G	Em	Am
	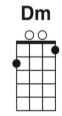	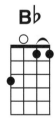	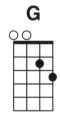	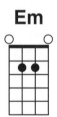	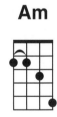

Banjo

C	F	Dm	B♭	G	Em	Am
		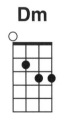		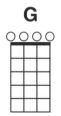	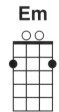	

God Bless the U.S.A.

Words and Music by Lee Greenwood

Standard Ukulele

D	G	A
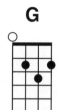	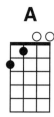	

Baritone Ukulele

D	G	A
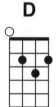	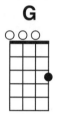	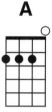

Guitar

D	G	A
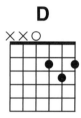	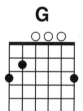	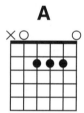

Mandolin

D	G	A
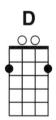	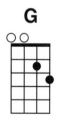	

Banjo

D	G	A
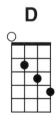	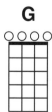	

A Good Hearted Woman

Words and Music by Willie Nelson and Waylon Jennings

Additional Lyrics

2. He likes the bright lights, the nightlife and good-timin' friends,
And when the party's all over she'll welcome him back home again.
Lord knows, she don't understand him, but she does the best that she can,
This good-hearted woman lovin' her good-timin' man.

Standard Ukulele

E	A	B7	F#m

Baritone Ukulele

E	A	B7	F#m

Guitar

E	A	B7	F#m

Mandolin

E	A	B7	F#m

Banjo

E	A	B7	F#m

Grandpa (Tell Me 'Bout the Good Old Days)

Words and Music by Jamie O'Hara

Standard Ukulele

G	C	D
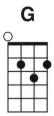	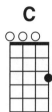	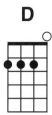

Baritone Ukulele

G	C	D
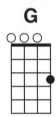		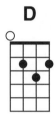

Guitar

G	C	D
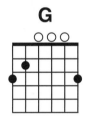	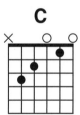	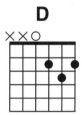

Mandolin

G	C	D
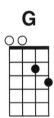	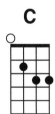	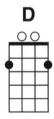

Banjo

G	C	D
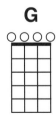	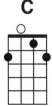	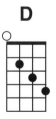

Green Green Grass of Home

Words and Music by Curly Putman

Additional Lyrics

2. The old house is still standing,
Though the paint is cracked and dry,
And there's that old oak tree that I used to play on.
Down the lane I'd walk with my sweet Mary,
Hair of gold and lips like cherries.
It's good to touch the green, green grass of home.

3. *Spoken:* Then I awake and look around me
At these four gray walls that surround me,
And I realize that I was only dreaming,
For there's a guard and there's a sad old padre.
Arm in arm, we'll walk at daybreak,
And again I'll touch the green, green grass of home.

Standard Ukulele

G	G#°7	D7	G7	C	E7	A7	Am

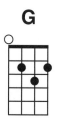    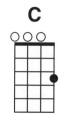   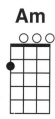

Baritone Ukulele

G	G#°7	D7	G7	C	E7	A7	Am

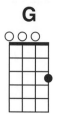   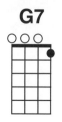    

Guitar

G	G#°7	D7	G7	C	E7	A7	Am

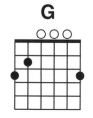 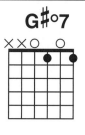 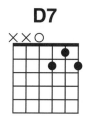 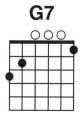   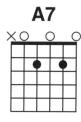 

Mandolin

G	G#°7	D7	G7	C	E7	A7	Am

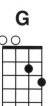 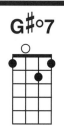  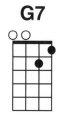  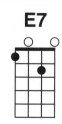  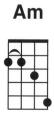

Banjo

G	G#°7	D7	G7	C	E7	A7	Am

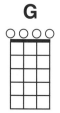 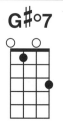  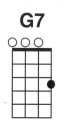 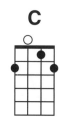   

Happy Trails

from the Television Series THE ROY ROGERS SHOW
Words and Music by Dale Evans

Verse

Moderately

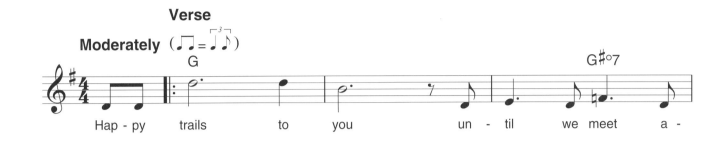

Hap - py trails to you un - til we meet a -

gain. Hap - py trails to you; keep

smil - ing un - til then. Who cares a - bout the clouds when we're to -

geth - er. Just sing a song and bring the sun - ny

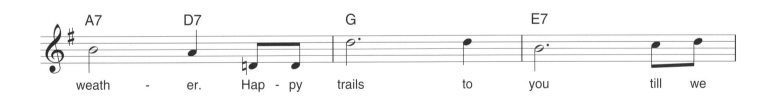

weath - er. Hap - py trails to you till we

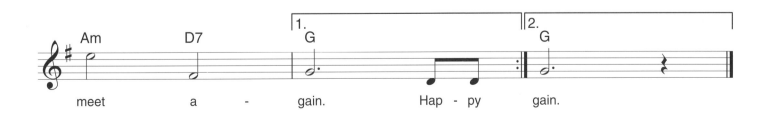

meet a - gain. Hap - py gain.

Standard Ukulele

G	C	D
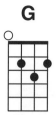	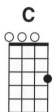	

Baritone Ukulele

G	C	D
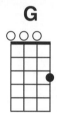		

Guitar

G	C	D
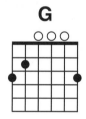	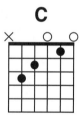	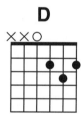

Mandolin

G	C	D
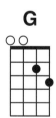	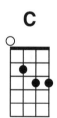	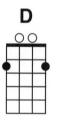

Banjo

G	C	D
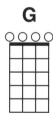		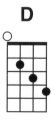

He Stopped Loving Her Today

Words and Music by Bobby Braddock and Curly Putman

Standard Ukulele

A	D	E
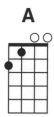	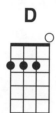	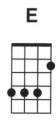

Baritone Ukulele

A	D	E
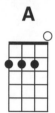		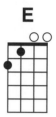

Guitar

A	D	E
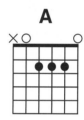	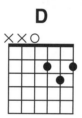	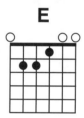

Mandolin

A	D	E
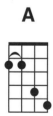	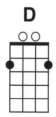	

Banjo

A	D	E
	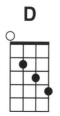	

Heartaches by the Number

Words and Music by Harlan Howard

Standard Ukulele

G	C	D	G7	A

Baritone Ukulele

G	C	D	G7	A

Guitar

G	C	D	G7	A
		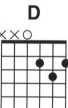		

Mandolin

G	C	D	G7	A
			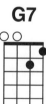	

Banjo

G	C	D	G7	A

Help Me Make It Through the Night

Words and Music by Kris Kristofferson

1.Take the rib-bon from my hair, shake it loose and let it
side till the ear-ly morn-ing
gone and to-mor-row's out of

fall, lay-in' soft a-gainst your skin,
light. All I'm tak-ing is your time.
sight, and it's sad to be a-lone.

like the shad-ows on the wall. 2. Come and lay down by my

Help me make it through the night.
Help me make it through the night.
I don't care what's right or

Bridge

wrong, and I won't try to un-der-stand.

Let the dev-il take to-mor-row. Lord, to-night I

need a friend. 3.Yes-ter-day is dead and

I don't want to be a-

lone. Help me make it through the night.

Standard Ukulele

C	D	G7	C7	F
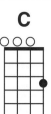		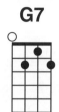	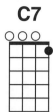	

Baritone Ukulele

C	D	G7	C7	F
		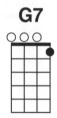		

Guitar

C	D	G7	C7	F
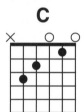		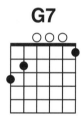	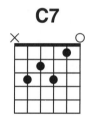	

Mandolin

C	D	G7	C7	F
	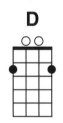			

Banjo

C	D	G7	C7	F
	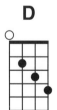	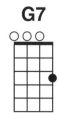		

Hey, Good Lookin'
Words and Music by Hank Williams

Standard Ukulele

E	B7	A	E7

Baritone Ukulele

E	B7	A	E7

Guitar

E	B7	A	E7
		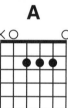	

Mandolin

E	B7	A	E7

Banjo

E	B7	A	E7

I Can't Help It (If I'm Still in Love with You)

Words and Music by Hank Williams

Standard Ukulele

F	C	G7	C7	D7
	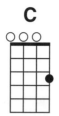	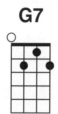	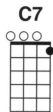	

Baritone Ukulele

F	C	G7	C7	D7
	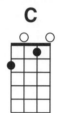	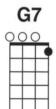		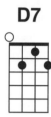

Guitar

F	C	G7	C7	D7
	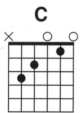	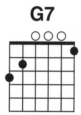	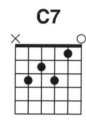	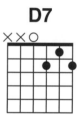

Mandolin

F	C	G7	C7	D7
	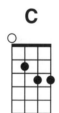	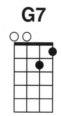		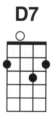

Banjo

F	C	G7	C7	D7
		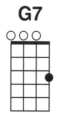		

I Can't Stop Loving You

Words and Music by Don Gibson

Standard Ukulele

G	C	D	D♭
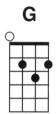	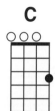	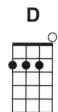	

Baritone Ukulele

G	C	D	D♭
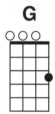	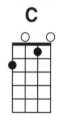		

Guitar

G	C	D	D♭
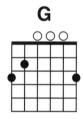	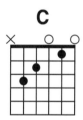	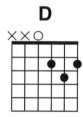	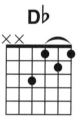

Mandolin

G	C	D	D♭
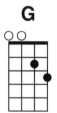	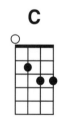		

Banjo

G	C	D	D♭
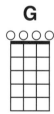	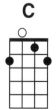	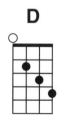	

I Fall to Pieces

Words and Music by Hank Cochran and Harlan Howard

Standard Ukulele

C	F	G	Am	Gsus4	D7	Em	Dm

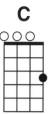   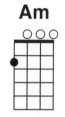 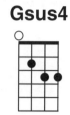  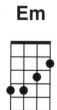 

Baritone Ukulele

C	F	G	Am	Gsus4	D7	Em	Dm

    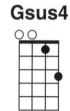   

Guitar

C	F	G	Am	Gsus4	D7	Em	Dm

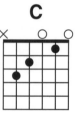  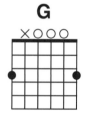     

Mandolin

C	F	G	Am	Gsus4	D7	Em	Dm

  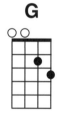 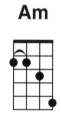 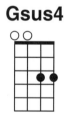 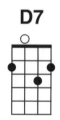  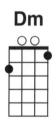

Banjo

C	F	G	Am	Gsus4	D7	Em	Dm

  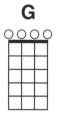  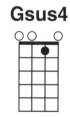 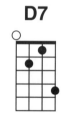 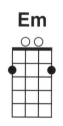 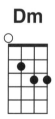

I Swear
Words and Music by Frank Myers and Gary Baker

Standard Ukulele

B7	E	A

Baritone Ukulele

B7	E	A
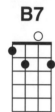	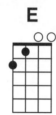	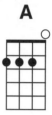

Guitar

B7	E	A
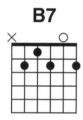	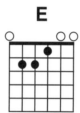	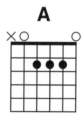

Mandolin

B7	E	A
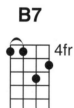	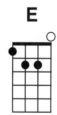	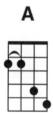

Banjo

B7	E	A
	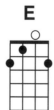	

I Walk the Line

Words and Music by John R. Cash

Standard Ukulele

G	Em	C	D
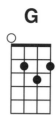		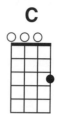	

Baritone Ukulele

G	Em	C	D
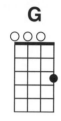	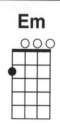	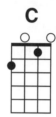	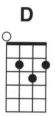

Guitar

G	Em	C	D
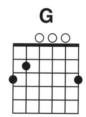	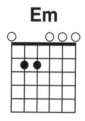	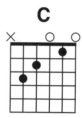	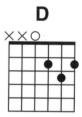

Mandolin

G	Em	C	D
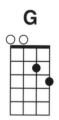	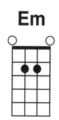	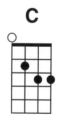	

Banjo

G	Em	C	D
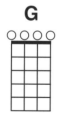	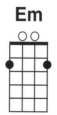	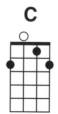	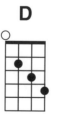

I Will Always Love You

Words and Music by Dolly Parton

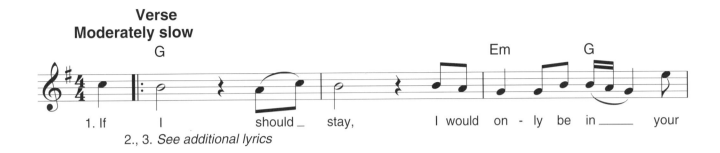

Verse
Moderately slow

1. If I should stay, I would on - ly be in your

2., 3. *See additional lyrics*

way. So I'll go, but I know I'll

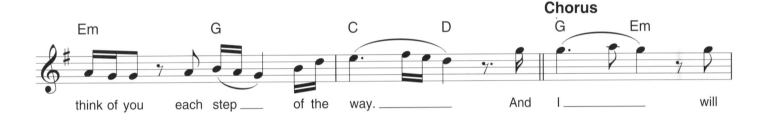

think of you each step of the way. And I will

Chorus

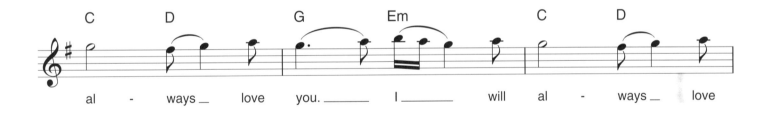

al - ways love you. I will al - ways love

you. 2. Bit - ter -

Additional Lyrics

2. Bittersweet memories,
   That's all I am taking with me.
   Goodbye, please don't cry.
   We both know that I'm not what you need.

3. *Spoken:* I hope life treats you kind,
   And I hope that you have all that you ever dreamed of.
   And I wish you joy and happiness,
   Sung: But above all of this I wish you love.

Standard Ukulele

G	Gmaj7	Em	Am	D7sus4	C

Baritone Ukulele

G	Gmaj7	Em	Am	D7sus4	C

Guitar

G	Gmaj7	Em	Am	D7sus4	C

Mandolin

G	Gmaj7	Em	Am	D7sus4	C

Banjo

G	Gmaj7	Em	Am	D7sus4	C

I.O.U.
Words and Music by Kerry Chater and Austin Roberts

Standard Ukulele

A	D	E
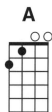	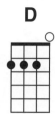	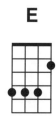

Baritone Ukulele

A	D	E
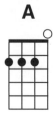	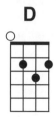	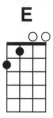

Guitar

A	D	E
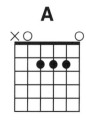	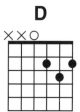	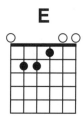

Mandolin

A	D	E
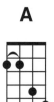	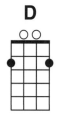	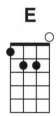

Banjo

A	D	E
	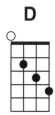	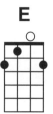

It Wasn't God Who Made Honky Tonk Angels

Words and Music by J.D. Miller

Standard Ukulele

C	Am	F	F♯	G	C7
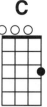	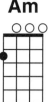				

Baritone Ukulele

C	Am	F	F♯	G	C7

Guitar

C	Am	F	F♯	G	C7

Mandolin

C	Am	F	F♯	G	C7

Banjo

C	Am	F	F♯	G	C7

It's Only Make Believe

Words and Music by Conway Twitty and Jack Nance

Standard Ukulele

C 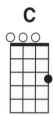 G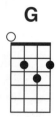

Baritone Ukulele

C  G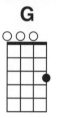

Guitar

C 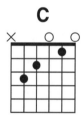 G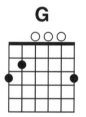

Mandolin

C 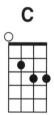 G

Banjo

C 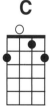 G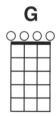

Jambalaya
(On the Bayou)
Words and Music by Hank Williams

Standard Ukulele

A	E7	D
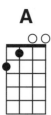	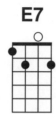	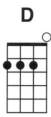

Baritone Ukulele

A	E7	D
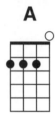	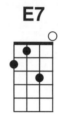	

Guitar

A	E7	D
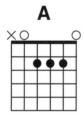	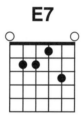	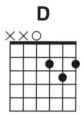

Mandolin

A	E7	D
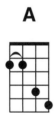	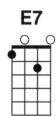	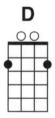

Banjo

A	E7	D
	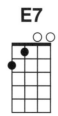	

Jealous Heart

Words and Music by Jenny Lou Carson

Verse

Moderately, in 2

1. Jeal - ous   heart,   oh,   jeal - ous   heart,   stop   beat - ing.
2., 3. *See additional lyrics*

Can't you   see   the   dam - age   you   have   done?   You have

driv - en   her   a - way   for - ev - er.   Jeal - ous   heart,   now

I'm   the   lone - ly   one.   I   was   part   of   ev - 'ry - thing she

planned for,   and   I   know   she   loved   me   at   the   start.

Now   she   hates   the   sight   of   all   I   stand for,   all   be -

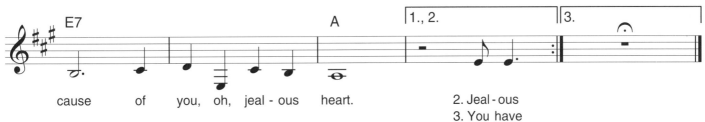

cause   of   you,   oh,   jeal - ous   heart.

[1., 2.]

2. Jeal - ous

[3.]

3. You have

Additional Lyrics

2. Jealous heart, why did I let you rule me
   When I knew the end would bring me pain?
   Now she's gone, she's gone and found another.
   Oh, I'll never see my love again.
   Through the years her memory will haunt me,
   Even though we're many miles apart.
   It's so hard to know she'll never want me,
   'Cause she heard your beating jealous heart.

3. You have filled my conscience full of sorrow,
   For I know she never was untrue.
   Jealous heart, why did you make her hate me?
   Now there's nothing left for jealous you.
   Many times I trusted you to guide me.
   But your guiding only brought me tears.
   Why, oh why, must I have you inside me,
   Jealous heart, for all my lonely years?

81

Standard Ukulele

C	F	G
		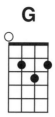

Baritone Ukulele

C	F	G
		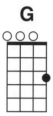

Guitar

C	F	G
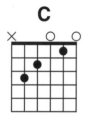	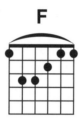	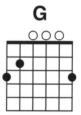

Mandolin

C	F	G
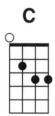		

Banjo

C	F	G
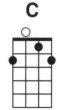		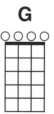

King of the Road
Words and Music by Roger Miller

Standard Ukulele

E	A	B7

Baritone Ukulele

E	A	B7

Guitar

E	A	B7

Mandolin

E	A	B7

Banjo

E	A	B7

Kiss an Angel Good Mornin'

Words and Music by Ben Peters

Verse
Moderately fast

1. When-ev-er I chance to meet ___ some old friends ___ on the ___ street, ___
peo-ple may try to guess ___ the se-cret of hap-pi - ness, ___

___ they won-der how does a man ___ get to be this ___ way. ___
___ but some of them nev - er learn ___ that it's a sim-ple ___ thing. ___

I've al-ways got a smil-in' ___ face ___
The se-cret I'm speak-in' ___ of ___ is a

an - y - time and an - y - place. ___ And ev - 'ry time they ask me why, ___
wom-an and a man in ___ love. ___ And the an-swer is in this song ___

Chorus

___ I just smile and ___ say: ___ } You've got to kiss an an-gel good morn-
___ that I al - ways ___ sing: ___ }

- in' and let her know you think a-bout her when you're ___ gone. ___

Kiss an an-gel good morn - in' and love her like the dev - il when you

get back ___ home. ___

2. Well,

Standard Ukulele

G	D7	C	G7	Am

Baritone Ukulele

G	D7	C	G7	Am

Guitar

G	D7	C	G7	Am

Mandolin

G	D7	C	G7	Am
	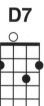	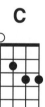		

Banjo

G	D7	C	G7	Am

The Last Word in Lonesome Is Me

Words and Music by Roger Miller

Standard Ukulele

Dm7	G7	C	F

Baritone Ukulele

Dm7	G7	C	F

Guitar

Dm7	G7	C	F

Mandolin

Dm7	G7	C	F

Banjo

Dm7	G7	C	F

Make the World Go Away

Words and Music by Hank Cochran

Standard Ukulele

D    **G** 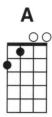   **A**

Baritone Ukulele

D    **G** 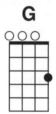   **A**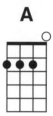

Guitar

D 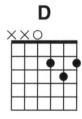   **G** 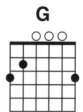   **A**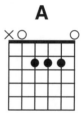

Mandolin

D 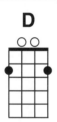   **G** 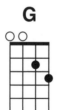   **A**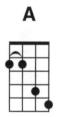

Banjo

D 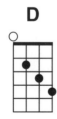   **G** 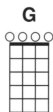   **A**

Mammas Don't Let Your Babies Grow Up to Be Cowboys

Words and Music by Ed Bruce and Patsy Bruce

Verse
Moderately slow, in 1

1. Cow-boys ain't eas-y to love, and they're hard-er to hold.
2. Cow-boys like smok-y old pool-rooms and clear moun-tain morn-ings,

They'd rath-er give you a song than dia-monds or gold.
lit-tle warm pup-pies and chil-dren and girls of the night.

Lone Star belt buck-les and old fad-ed Le-vi's and each night be-
Them that don't know him won't like him, and them that do some-times won't

gins a new day. If you don't un-der-stand him and
know how to take him. He ain't wrong, he's just dif-f'rent, but his

he don't die young, he'll prob-'ly just ride a-way.
pride won't let him do things to make you think he's right.

Chorus

Mam-mas, don't let your ba - bies grow up to be cow-boys.

Don't let 'em pick gui-tars and drive them old trucks. Let 'em be
'Cause they nev-er stay home and they're al-ways a-lone, e-ven with

1.
D.C. al Fine (take repeat)

doc-tors and law-yers and such.
some-one they

2. **Fine**
love.

Standard Ukulele

D	A7	D7	G	A	E7
	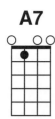			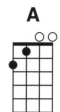	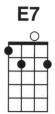

Baritone Ukulele

D	A7	D7	G	A	E7
			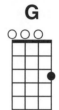	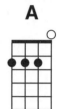	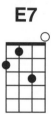

Guitar

D	A7	D7	G	A	E7
	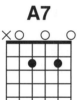	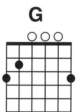	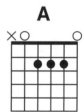	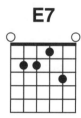	

Mandolin

D	A7	D7	G	A	E7
		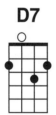	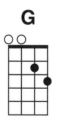	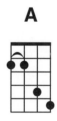	

Banjo

D	A7	D7	G	A	E7
					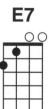

Oh, Lonesome Me

Words and Music by Don Gibson

Standard Ukulele

D  **A7**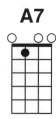

Baritone Ukulele

D  **A7**

Guitar

D 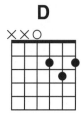 **A7**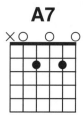

Mandolin

D 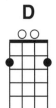 **A7**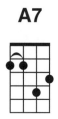

Banjo

D 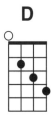 **A7**

Okie from Muskogee

Words and Music by Merle Haggard and Roy Edward Burris

Standard Ukulele

G	B7	Am	C	D

Baritone Ukulele

G	B7	Am	C	D

Guitar

G	B7	Am	C	D

Mandolin

G	B7	Am	C	D
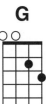			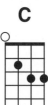	

Banjo

G	B7	Am	C	D

On the Road Again

Words and Music by Willie Nelson

Standard Ukulele

G	C	D
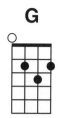	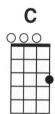	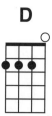

Baritone Ukulele

G	C	D
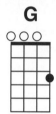		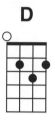

Guitar

G	C	D
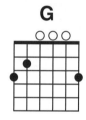	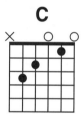	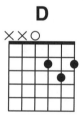

Mandolin

G	C	D
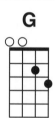	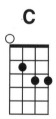	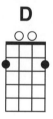

Banjo

G	C	D
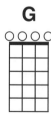		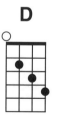

Release Me

Words and Music by Robert Yount, Eddie Miller and Dub Williams

Standard Ukulele

G	C	D7
	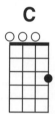	

Baritone Ukulele

G	C	D7
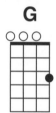	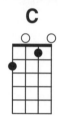	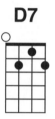

Guitar

G	C	D7
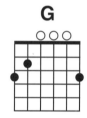	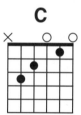	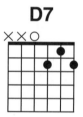

Mandolin

G	C	D7
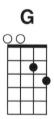	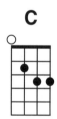	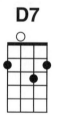

Banjo

G	C	D7
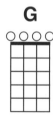	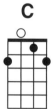	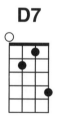

Ring of Fire

Words and Music by Merle Kilgore and June Carter

Standard Ukulele

C	F	Am	G	B♭
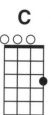	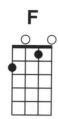	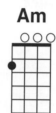		

Baritone Ukulele

C	F	Am	G	B♭
			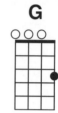	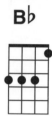

Guitar

C	F	Am	G	B♭
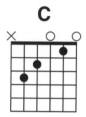	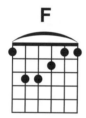	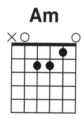	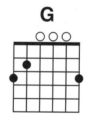	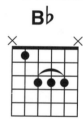

Mandolin

C	F	Am	G	B♭
		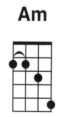	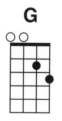	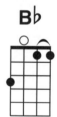

Banjo

C	F	Am	G	B♭
			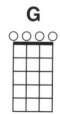	

Rocky Top

Words and Music by Boudleaux Bryant and Felice Bryant

Standard Ukulele

E	A	B7

Baritone Ukulele

E	A	B7

Guitar

E	A	B7

Mandolin

E	A	B7

Banjo

E	A	B7

Send Me the Pillow You Dream On

Words and Music by Hank Locklin

Verse
Moderately

1. Send me the pil - low that you dream on. _____
2. Send me the pil - low that you dream on. _____

Don't you know that I still care for you? _____
May - be time will let our dreams come true. _____

Send me the pil - low that you dream on, _____ so,

dar - ling, I ___ can dream on it too. _____ { Each
                                                    { I've

night while I'm sleep-ing, oh, so lone - ly, _____ I'll
wait - ed so long for you to write me, _____ but

share your love in dreams that once were true. _____
just a mem - 'ry's all that's left of you. _____

Send me the pil - low that you dream on, _____ so,

dar - ling, I ___ can dream on it too. _____

Standard Ukulele

E	A7	B7

Baritone Ukulele

E	A7	B7

Guitar

E	A7	B7
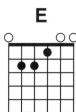		

Mandolin

E	A7	B7

Banjo

E	A7	B7

Singing the Blues

Words and Music by Melvin Endsley

Standard Ukulele

Em   **Em7**   **C**   **B7**   **Am**

Baritone Ukulele

Em   **Em7**   **C**   **B7**   **Am**

Guitar

Em   **Em7**   **C**   **B7**   **Am**

Mandolin

Em   **Em7**   **C**   **B7**   **Am**

Banjo

Em   **Em7**   **C**   **B7**   **Am**

Sixteen Tons
Words and Music by Merle Travis

Verse

1. Some peo-ple say a man is made out of mud. A poor man's made out of
2., 3., 4. *See additional lyrics*

mus-cle and blood, mus-cle and blood and skin and bones, a

mind that's a weak and a back that's strong. You load six - teen tons,

Chorus

what do you get? An - oth-er day old-er and deep-er in debt. Saint

Pe - ter, don't you call me 'cause I can't go. I owe my soul to the

1., 2., 3.
com-pa-ny store.

2. I _____ was
3. I _____ was
4. If _____ you

4.
com-pa-ny store.

Additional Lyrics

2. I was born one mornin' when the sun didn't shine.
   I picked up my shovel and I walked to the mine.
   I loaded sixteen tons of number nine coal,
   And the straw boss said, "Well, bless my soul."

3. I was born one mornin', it was drizzlin' rain.
   Fightin' and trouble are my middle name.
   I was raised in the canebrake by an ol' mama lion.
   Can't no high-toned woman make me walk the line.

4. If you see me comin', better step aside.
   A lotta men didn't, a lotta men died.
   One fist of iron, the other of steel,
   If the right one don't get you, then the left one will.

Standard Ukulele

Em	C	G	D	Am	Bm

Baritone Ukulele

Em	C	G	D	Am	Bm

Guitar

Em	C	G	D	Am	Bm

Mandolin

Em	C	G	D	Am	Bm
	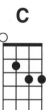		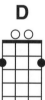		

Banjo

Em	C	G	D	Am	Bm

Smoky Mountain Rain

Words and Music by Dennis Morgan and Kye Fleming

Standard Ukulele

G	Bm	Am	D	C

Baritone Ukulele

G	Bm	Am	D	C

Guitar

G	Bm	Am	D	C

Mandolin

G	Bm	Am	D	C
	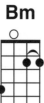			

Banjo

G	Bm	Am	D	C

Snowbird

Words and Music by Gene MacLellan

Verse
Moderately, in 2

1. Be-neath ___ this snow-y man-tle cold ___ and _____ clean, the un-
2.-5. *See additional lyrics*

- born grass lies wait-ing for its coat ___ to turn ___ to green. ___ The snow-

- bird sings the song ___ he al-ways _____ sings and speaks to me ___ of flow-

- ers that will bloom a-gain ___ in _____ spring.

1.–4. 2. When I ___
4. The

5. Yeah, ___ if I could, ___ you know ___ that I ___ would fly _____

a-way ___ with you. _____

Additional Lyrics

2. When I was young, my heart was young then too.
   Anything that it would tell me, that's the thing that I would do.
   But now I feel such emptiness within,
   For the thing that I want most in life's the thing that I can't win.

3., 5. Spread your tiny wings and fly away,
   And take the snow back with you where it came from on that day.
   The one I love forever is untrue,
   And if I could, you know that I would fly away with you.

4. The breeze along the river seems to say
   That he'll only break my heart again should I decide to stay.
   So little snowbird take me with you when you go
   To that land of gentle breezes where the peaceful waters flow.

Standard Ukulele

C	A7	D7	Fmaj7	Em7	G7

Baritone Ukulele

C	A7	D7	Fmaj7	Em7	G7

Guitar

C	A7	D7	Fmaj7	Em7	G7

   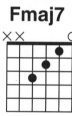

Mandolin

C	A7	D7	Fmaj7	Em7	G7

Banjo

C	A7	D7	Fmaj7	Em7	G7

Southern Nights

Words and Music by Allen Toussaint

Verse
Moderately

1. South - ern __ nights, __ have you ev - er felt a South - ern __ night? __
2., 3. *See additional lyrics*

Free as a breeze, __ not to men - tion the trees, __ whis - tling

tunes that you know __ and love so. __ South - ern __ nights, __

just as good e - ven when closed your __ eyes. __ I __ a -

To Coda ⊕

pol - o - gize __ to an - y - one who can tru - ly say __ that he has

2nd time, D.C. al Coda

found a bet - ter way. __

⊕ **Coda**

in the South - ern skies. __

Additional Lyrics

2. Southern skies, have you ever noticed Southern skies?
Its precious beauty lies just beyond the eye.
It goes running through your soul like the stories told of old.
Old man, he and his dog that walked the old land.
Every flower touched his cold hand.
As he slowly walked by, weeping willows would cry for joy.

3. Feel so good, feel so good it's frightening.
Wish I could stop this world from fighting.
La, da, da, da, da, da, la, da, da, da, da, da,
Da, da, da, da, da, da, da, da, da, da, da.
Mysteries like this and many others in the trees
Blow in the night in the Southern skies.

Standard Ukulele

C	G7	Dm	F	D7	E7	A7
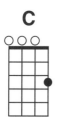						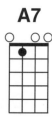

Baritone Ukulele

C	G7	Dm	F	D7	E7	A7
	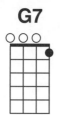			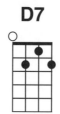	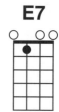	

Guitar

C	G7	Dm	F	D7	E7	A7
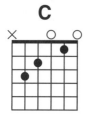	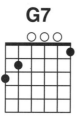	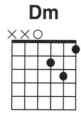			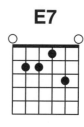	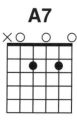

Mandolin

C	G7	Dm	F	D7	E7	A7
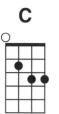	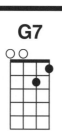	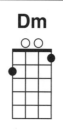				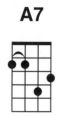

Banjo

C	G7	Dm	F	D7	E7	A7
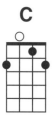	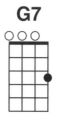	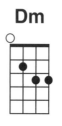			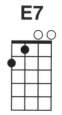	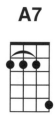

Stand by Your Man

Words and Music by Tammy Wynette and Billy Sherrill

Standard Ukulele

G	A7	D7	C	Em

Baritone Ukulele

G	A7	D7	C	Em

Guitar

G	A7	D7	C	Em

Mandolin

G	A7	D7	C	Em

Banjo

G	A7	D7	C	Em

Sweet Dreams

Words and Music by Don Gibson

Standard Ukulele

G	Em	D	C	F

Baritone Ukulele

G	Em	D	C	F

Guitar

G	Em	D	C	F

Mandolin

G	Em	D	C	F
		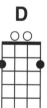	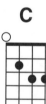	

Banjo

G	Em	D	C	F

Take Me Home, Country Roads

Words and Music by John Denver, Bill Danoff and Taffy Nivert

Standard Ukulele

D	A7	D7	G	E7
	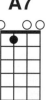			

Baritone Ukulele

D	A7	D7	G	E7

Guitar

D	A7	D7	G	E7

Mandolin

D	A7	D7	G	E7
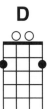				

Banjo

D	A7	D7	G	E7

Take These Chains from My Heart

Words and Music by Fred Rose and Hy Heath

Standard Ukulele

G	G7	C	D7	B7

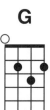    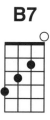

Baritone Ukulele

G	G7	C	D7	B7

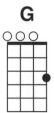 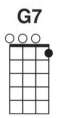  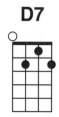 

Guitar

G	G7	C	D7	B7

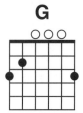 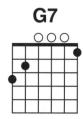 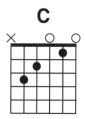  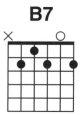

Mandolin

G	G7	C	D7	B7

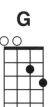   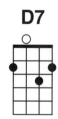 

Banjo

G	G7	C	D7	B7

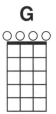 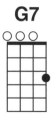  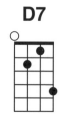 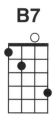

Tennessee Waltz

Words and Music by Redd Stewart and Pee Wee King

Standard Ukulele

G	Am	D7sus4	D7	C

Baritone Ukulele

G	Am	D7sus4	D7	C

Guitar

G	Am	D7sus4	D7	C
		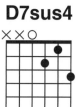		

Mandolin

G	Am	D7sus4	D7	C

Banjo

G	Am	D7sus4	D7	C

To All the Girls I've Loved Before

Words by Hal David
Music by Albert Hammond

Standard Ukulele

F	E	C	G7	C7	D7
	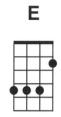	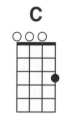	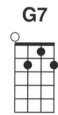	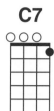	

Baritone Ukulele

F	E	C	G7	C7	D7
		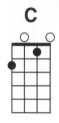	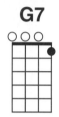		

Guitar

F	E	C	G7	C7	D7
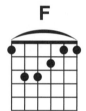	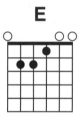	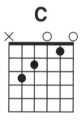	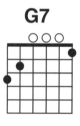	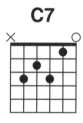	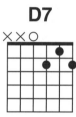

Mandolin

F	E	C	G7	C7	D7
	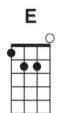				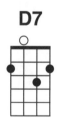

Banjo

F	E	C	G7	C7	D7
	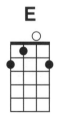		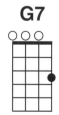		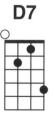

Tumbling Tumbleweeds

Words and Music by Bob Nolan

Standard Ukulele

C	F	G	C7
	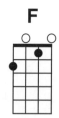	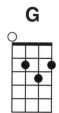	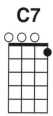

Baritone Ukulele

C	F	G	C7
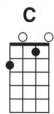		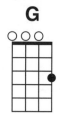	

Guitar

C	F	G	C7
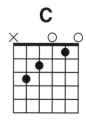		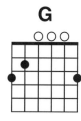	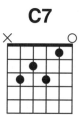

Mandolin

C	F	G	C7
			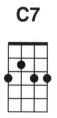

Banjo

C	F	G	C7
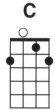		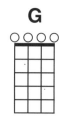	

Walkin' After Midnight

Lyrics by Don Hecht
Music by Alan W. Block

Standard Ukulele

C	F	G
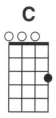	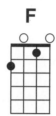	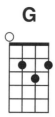

Baritone Ukulele

C	F	G
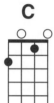		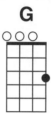

Guitar

C	F	G
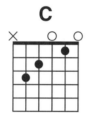	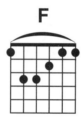	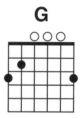

Mandolin

C	F	G
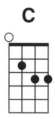		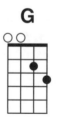

Banjo

C	F	G
		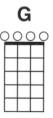

Walking the Floor Over You

Words and Music by Ernest Tubb

Standard Ukulele

G	Am7	D7sus4	C	D	Em7	Bm7

Baritone Ukulele

G	Am7	D7sus4	C	D	Em7	Bm7

Guitar

G	Am7	D7sus4	C	D	Em7	Bm7

Mandolin

G	Am7	D7sus4	C	D	Em7	Bm7

  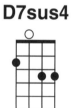 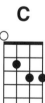 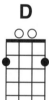

Banjo

G	Am7	D7sus4	C	D	Em7	Bm7

What's Forever For
Words and Music by Rafe Van Hoy

Verse
Moderately slow

1. I've been look-ing at peo - ple
2. May-be it's me who's gone cra - zy,
3. And I see love-hun-gry peo - ple

and how they change with the times, ___
but I can't un-der-stand why ___
try-ing their best to sur-vive, ___

and late-ly all ___ I've been
all these lov - ers keep
when right there in their hands ___ is a

see-ing are peo-ple ___ throw-ing love a-way ___ and los-ing their minds. ___
hurt-ing each oth-er ___ when good love is so hard to come by. ___
dy-ing ro-mance, ___ and they're not e-ven try'ng to keep it a-live. ___

Chorus

So what's the glo - ry in liv - ing? Does - n't

an - y - bod - y ev - er stay to - geth - er an - y - more? ___

To Coda

And if love ___ nev - er lasts for - ev - er, tell me, ___ what's for - ev - er for? ___

D.C. al Coda
(no repeat)

Coda

what's for - ev - er for? ___

Standard Ukulele

G5	C	D	G	Em
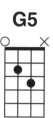	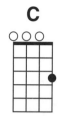		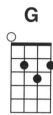	

Baritone Ukulele

G5	C	D	G	Em
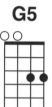			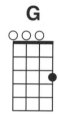	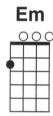

Guitar

G5	C	D	G	Em
	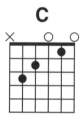	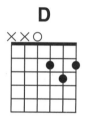	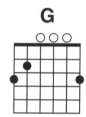	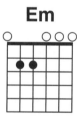

Mandolin

G5	C	D	G	Em
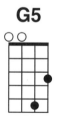	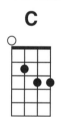	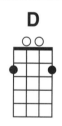	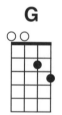	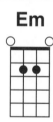

Banjo

G5	C	D	G	Em
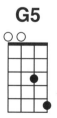			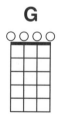	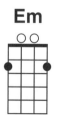

When Will I Be Loved

Words and Music by Phil Everly

Standard Ukulele

D	A	G
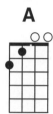	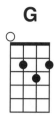	

Baritone Ukulele

D	A	G
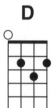		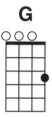

Guitar

D	A	G
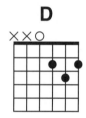	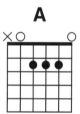	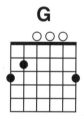

Mandolin

D	A	G
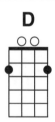	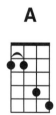	

Banjo

D	A	G
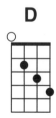		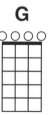

When You Say Nothing at All

Words and Music by Don Schlitz and Paul Overstreet

Standard Ukulele

D	G	A	Em7

Baritone Ukulele

D	G	A	Em7
	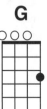		

Guitar

D	G	A	Em7
	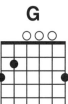		

Mandolin

D	G	A	Em7

Banjo

D	G	A	Em7

You're Still the One

Words and Music by Shania Twain and R.J. Lange

Standard Ukulele

C	F	G7	D7
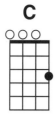	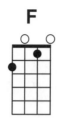		

Baritone Ukulele

C	F	G7	D7
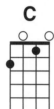		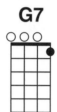	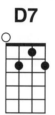

Guitar

C	F	G7	D7
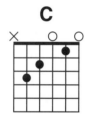	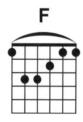	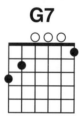	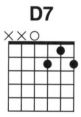

Mandolin

C	F	G7	D7
	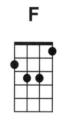	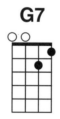	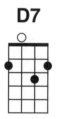

Banjo

C	F	G7	D7
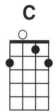		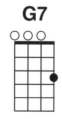	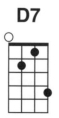

Your Cheatin' Heart

Words and Music by Hank Williams

Moderately slow, in 2

Chorus

1. Your cheat - in' ___ heart will make you weep.
heart will pine some - day

You'll cry and cry and try to sleep. But sleep _ won't _
and crave the love you threw a - way. The time _ will _

come the whole night through. Your cheat - in' heart
come when you'll be blue.

will tell on you. When tears come down like fall - in'

rain, you'll toss a - round and call my name.

You'll walk _ the _ floor the way I do. Your cheat - in'

heart will tell on you. 2. Your cheat - in' ___

Tuning

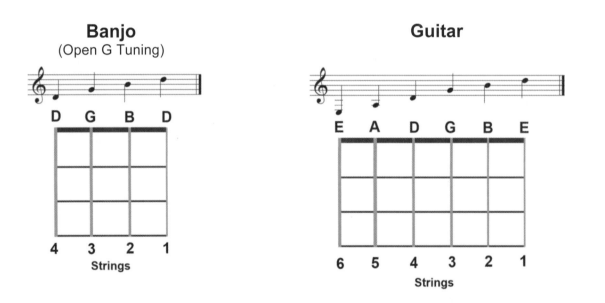

Standard Ukulele
(Soprano, Concert, Tenor)

G C E A

4 3 2 1
Strings

Baritone Ukulele

D G B E

4 3 2 1
Strings

Mandolin

G D A E

4 3 2 1
Strings

Banjo
(Open G Tuning)

D G B D

4 3 2 1
Strings

Guitar

E A D G B E

6 5 4 3 2 1
Strings

All banjo chord formations illustrated in this book are based on "Open G" tuning. If an alternate tuning is used the banjo player can read the chord letters for the songs and disregard the diagrams.